5 WAYS
TO EXPERIENCE AN
AMAZING CHRISTMAS

INTENSIFYING

THE SPIRIT

OF THE SEASON

by

Ami Keath

Copyright 2009
Ami Keath
All rights reserved
Only the portion of this publication that includes a questionnaire and craft list with craft instructions may be reproduced, stored in any electronic system, or transmitted in any form or by any means, electronic, mechanical, photocopy, recording or otherwise without written permission from the author. Brief quotations may be used in literary reviews.

Photo of author on front and back cover
by Jesse Keath (author's son)

Interior photos by Ami Keath

ISBN: 978-0-9820314-1-4

First Printing: December 2009

For Information Contact:
Enlightening Eyes, LLC
P.O. Box 258
Haslet, TX 76052

Or visit our website at
www.enlighteningeyes.com

Printed in the USA
Self-Published through createspace.com
Amazon.com

5 WAYS TO EXPERIENCE AN AMAZING CHRISTMAS

Introduction   7

First Way
    Discover and Display Hopes and Dreams -
    Focusing on you and members of your household   10

Second Way
    Enhance the Splendor of Your Surroundings with
    Lights – Focusing on you and your neighbors   19

Third Way
    Reach Out to the Ones That Tug on Your Heart –
    Focusing on those less fortunate   27

Fourth Way
    Compile Calendars and Create Crafts –
    Focusing on extended family, friends and children   34

Fifth Way
    Honor Saint Nicholas Properly
    And Restore the Innocence of the Spirit of the
    Season – Focusing on children and those who
    influence them   52

Get to Know the Real Provider
    Focusing on you and God   83

Which picture best describes your last Christmas?
Was it boring or maybe completely draining?

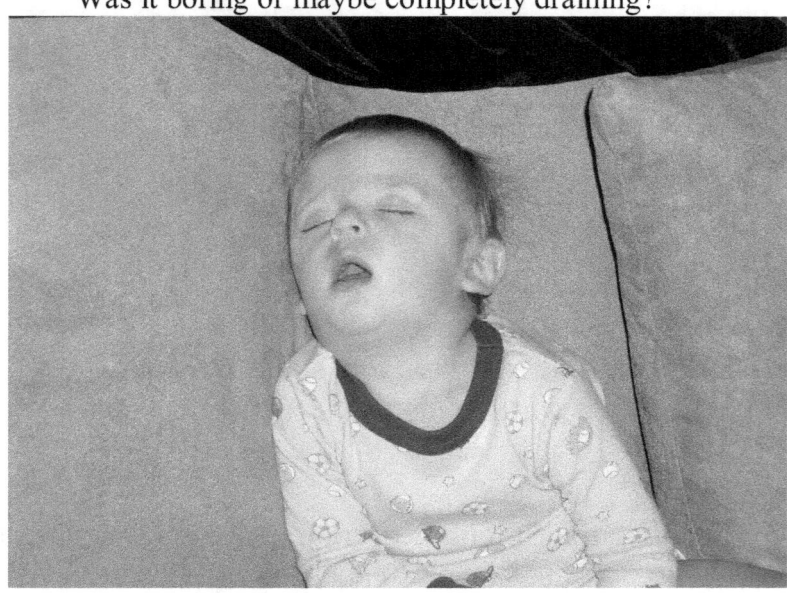

Or, was it packed with harmless fun, surrounded by family and friends making good memories?

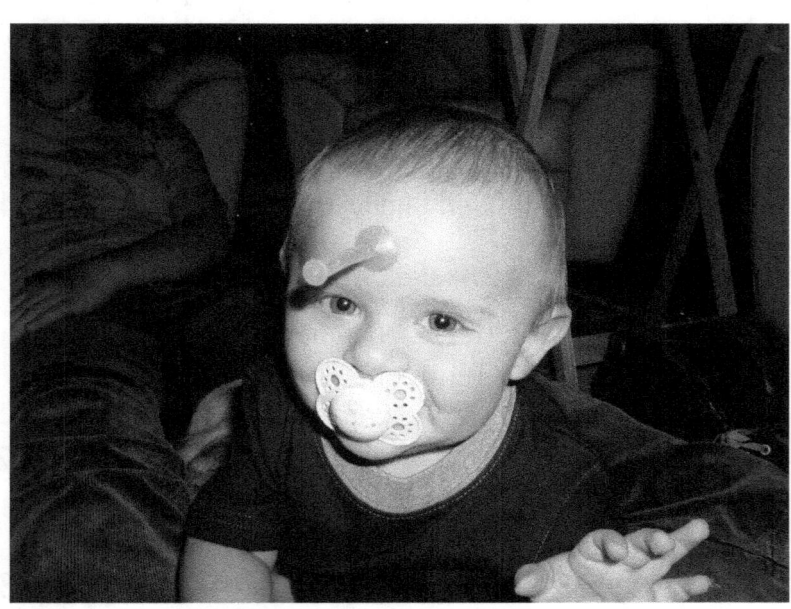

INTRODUCTION

Do you want your Christmas Season this year to explode with powerful memories and deeper friendships? Maybe last year you spent lots of money, ate up tons of time rearranging schedules and gave up several fun activities just to spend time with your family or friends and neighbors only to come away feeling just as distant and clueless of what was really going on in their hearts as before. Make that money, time, and sacrificed activities well worth it. Determine this year not to lose the focus of the reason for family and friend gatherings. Hopefully that reason is to share in each other's hopes and reconnect in an effort to keep up with what is going on in each other's lives. Being there together in person is far more memorable than just texting, emailing, face-booking, twittering or even phoning. Think of the deepest friendships you have and note how they got deep. Time spent with your friend, and an effort to show interest in what affected your friend, are two of the biggest things that strengthen a relationship. Way One and Way Four of this book deal heavily with this issue.

Does your current holiday tradition leave you with a better picture of your own life's goals? It may show a glimpse of what your current interest or hobby might be, but it falls far short of revealing the driving force that propels you to keep reaching for something more in life. What is it that really gets you excited? Do you have a set time each year when you really take a hard look at your life and narrow down what makes you tick? Way One will help get you started in defining who you are and what you were wired to do best. You can also apply it to others so that they can learn to know themselves more fully at the same time that you are getting to know them better.

Looking back each year after the Holiday is over, are there regrets that you did not make any effort to reach out to the lonely or struggling? Do not let that happen again. Let Way Three show you what you can do about that.

Are you tired of having to shop for just the right gift so that the recipient's disappointment does not get you depressed?

Buying presents for all the special people in your life all at one time gets to be a bit much. There are always those that feel left out or slighted by a lesser gift. Then there are those that waste hard-earned money on gifts that the recipient really does not like but does not want to admit it, so are stuck with to avoid hurt feelings. Does the joy or success of the holiday rest solely on the presents? Way Four outlines a method to skip all that. Besides that it reveals how the rest of the months of the year can be enriched by more attention given to other special occasions. Can you relate to this weary shopper massaging her sore foot?

This book just may be the answer to intensifying the Christmas Spirit that makes the season an amazing and wonderful experience as opposed to a hectic whirlwind of events that ends up becoming a source of weariness. The enlightening information enclosed offers five promising projects that when done with a sincere heart of passion and a fun-filled positive approach have the potential of shaping a life-changing set of new ways to celebrate the last month of each year.

The First Way:

Discover and Display Hopes and Dreams -
Focusing on you and members of your household

Here is a new project that you can introduce into your holiday season that will not only make this time of the year more special but it will help you get to know yourself better as well as help others get to know you better. If there are others in your household then each individual will want to participate in this process for themselves.

Let this be a Christmas season that stirs up the deep hidden dreams about your future that you have kept suppressed for lack of belief that they could come true. Set aside time to find a quiet place in which to probe the corners of your mind digging up memories or clues that reveal the things that really get you excited. Remove all limits in your thinking of what people have said you would never be able to do, where you thought you would never be able to go, and what you felt you could never afford. What was it that lit up your face and tugged at your heart? Maybe it was a talent that you once tinkered with, or a sport that invigorated you. Was there a career that seemed like it would have fulfilled your wildest dreams but you felt so incapable of ever achieving it? Do you notice times when you are watching the news that a certain issue gets you a lot more stirred up than any other? Write down all those thoughts tossed aside from your youth along with those that surfaced in more recent times.

To learn more about the subject of finding your strengths and your call in life here are a few really good books that I recommend:

Discovering Your Purpose, by Ivy Haley;
Now, Discover Your Strengths, by Marcus Buckingham & Donald O. Clifton, Ph. D. (www.simonsays.com);
The Path, Creating Your Mission Statement for Work and for Life, by Laurie Beth Jones (www.lauriebethjones.com);

God's Master Plan for Your Life, Ten Keys to Fulfilling Your Destiny, by Gloria Copeland (www.godsmasterplanforyourlife.com);

The 360 Degree Leader, Developing Your Influence from Anywhere in the Organization, by John C. Maxwell (www.maximumimpact.com).

These books are excellent tools that walk you through helpful ways of discovering your life's calling. Some of them provide helpful lists of things such as careers that match certain talents and skills, giving you a hint of what you would really be good at.

Notice below, some are creative with their hands to make pretty things while others just are not.

Compile these thoughts into a list of careers that you feel fit your dreams.

Next, narrow the list of careers down by crossing off those that made less of an impact on you. Weed out all but your top five.

1) What would you most like to do and be very good at doing?

2) What you would like to do almost as much as number one above?

3) What else would you still be thrilled to be doing even after long hours of working hard at it?

4) What else would you enjoy doing and still be pretty good at?

5) What would you like to do very much?

One final elimination is necessary to keep your project simple. Decide which two are your favorite vocations or activities.

Now what you are going to do with this information is build a miniature city or scene. If you have ever known someone who collected toy train sets as a hobby you may have noticed how they were usually built around a small village including trees, benches, a train depot and other miniature buildings such as post office, local food market, or even a church. This designing of a life-like miniature landscape/cityscape is the decorative and fun way to display the results of the research and discovery of each person's life calling.

Another part of this project is letting your personality come through in the way you set up the components of your scene. They do not have to be perfect. They do not have to be completely serious. Notice in the above archeological dig (flag says "Ancient Relic Site") that the men are unearthing a dinosaur skeleton all in one piece. The other dinosaur skeleton is watching in complete disbelief as is evidenced by his mouth gaping open. Meanwhile, people on the wild life reserve (flag says "Wild Life Reserve") are allowed to just mingle among the dangerous felines, petting them with little caution. It's ok though, because at the top center of the picture there sits a man crouched behind a barrier with a dart gun aimed and ready.

This picture above, set up on a counter top right over a kitchen sink, along with the picture on the next page, which was set up on the top of an old Singer sewing machine, are very small and simple examples of miniature scenes.

In fact, the picture on this page is just a snapshot of fictional movie characters in various poses. It represents the unfolding of an action packed adventure film. Is there a movie deep inside you that you have wanted to create or direct? This could be a first step in setting that goal into motion. When showcasing it to family and friends it may be discovered that you have true potential as a film maker. Let those ambitions that you feel are way too lofty for you come out on a miniature scale so that you can see them with your own eyes. Envisioning a dream helps it come closer to becoming reality in your life.

In case you are creative, you can cut costs by making your own buildings, trees and such using simple things around the house. For example, cover a rectangular box with tin foil to form a sky scraper; or twist three or four twisty ties together, branching them out at one end for branches and slightly separating them at the other end for roots to make a tree.

Chenille stems are a good choice for a variety of shapes. They make fluffy little animals, hats, trees, bushes, and so on. Those little plastic three-pronged things that you get in the pizza box when you have pizza delivered make good tables or stands. Straws stuck in styro-foam or play dough make good poles. Acquire some craft clay and use it to form animals, people, whatever you desire. Then after baking it just right, paint the creatures or shapes you made to fit perfectly what you want to have in your scene.

In the case that you are not one of those creative people then, make it a shopping adventure (if you so desire) to find just the right miniature pieces that represent the scene you are creating. You may want to divide the shopping list between family members to purchase as their gift for the year to each other. To avoid unwanted pieces provide the purchaser with the exact store or website from which your desired piece can be bought. These building blocks of the model of the person's dreams would be best gathered throughout the year and given at least a month ahead of time in order for the recipient to have time to prepare for this project.

Some may feel that this is too much of a self-centered project, yet this activity encourages a person to reach beyond what others say they could be good at or that they should focus on in their lives, to be self-expressive through what they themselves discover they are good at and should focus on. Furthermore, studies show that as a person finds their area of expertise or calling in the work force that they were born with strengths to do it energizes them despite the fact that the work may be hard. This ends up making them more productive as opposed to weary and drained at the end of each work day. As workers are more excited about their jobs or niche in society they become more beneficial to society. They are healthier and happier since the stress and strain is greatly reduced and even replaced by a sense of accomplishment and fulfillment. It is easier to reach out and love others when you first have confidence in yourself.

Do not feel like you have to limit this activity to just yourself. If you have ever had to say good-bye to a loved one, you know there comes a moment when you ask yourself, "While they were still alive could I have done something more to show them how I loved them?" Well, this is a solid way to show love.

Take the time to learn what really drives your loved ones to get out of bed each day and face the world. Try seeing things from their perspective. When you learn about your family members' and friends' strengths and callings it is fun to help them fulfill their dreams and build their miniature scenes at Christmas.

Let us use a family of four to be our sample family for this first project. Dad will be the owner/President of a large company in the center of a thriving metropolis. Mom will be the fashion designer/owner of a lucrative chain of women's apparel stores. Josh will be a famous baseball player/owner of an exotic wildlife reserve; while Jessica will be a pop-star singer/famous hair designer.

Based upon our sample family's information we will look for miniature items such as:

Buildings for Dad and Mom
Nice die cast cars for their transport
Maybe a nice die cast jet for travel
Some well-dressed female figurines to display Mom's talent
Some business-like male figurines for Dad
Some baseball figurines for Josh
A baseball field with stadium (constructed of anything you feel is suitable-
such as styro-foam carved into layered half-circles with several miniature lego figurines sitting on it to represent fans.)
A couple lions, tigers and any other animal Josh would desire to work with
A stage with lights for Jessica (again constructed of anything you feel suitable-
such as little boxes painted black for the sound system, miniature key- chain flash lights to be the spot lights elevated on a stick stuck in styro-foam)
Some figurines with instruments such as guitar, drums and keyboard
A couple salon chairs for Jessica

Some mini dolls with various hair color
Rolls of fluffy white batting for snow (it is supposed to be a Christmas scene)
Maybe a couple strings of lights to light up the display
Trees, benches, tan or gray ribbons to serve as walkways or roads
Small pebbles, mirrors to lay down for ponds on Josh's reserve

    Dad's scene may show a thriving city with restaurants, various businesses, schools, whatever he desires in his booming cityscape. It may include a luxury car or even private jet transporting him to his executive office marked with a sign.

    Mom's world of fashion is set forth with a couple miniature malls sporting a cat walk for fashion models and stores with her chain store name on them. She can even set up a red carpet awards show where her designs are the ones the stars are wearing for the evening.

    A small-scale baseball stadium and field would be the foundation for Josh's empire. Small pictures of Josh could double as posters revealing his popularity as Player of the Year. Close by a lush landscape would serve as a wild life refuge for his collection of exotic animals he has rescued from perilous destinies.

    The final career of the family is nestled neatly on top of the big speakers next to the television or stereo where music can bring the stage to life. Jessica's pop-star status is displayed with little home made head set microphones on Barbie dolls. Their hair and clothes charged with a wild flare to reflect her skill for unique designs.

    Each family member's scene can be tweaked to look as if it were the Christmas season by adding fake snow, Christmas lights, and any other miniscule holiday decorations.

    Each individual could have their own scene on one piece of furniture or they could all be blended together over a number of pieces of furniture. Do you have some counter top space right above your sink that separates your kitchen from your living room or breakfast nook? This would be a good place to develop a miniature scene. Do you have an antique Singer sewing machine that folds down leaving a flat surface? How about an old dresser that you could clear off just for the season to highlight your stature-reduced world? Does your entertainment center have a good sized shelf that could be made available for the December month? What about a coffee table or top of a china cabinet that never really gets used? For those without pets, your landscape could double as a tree skirt under a big beautiful Christmas tree that then shelters the replica of your personalized stage. These all would do nicely for a temporary construction site for your minuscule land in which you flourish. Get creative and have fun. This is your dream put on display for all to see and enjoy.

Here is a tip to get some extra help. Being one who believes in God, I have devoted my life to live the way that Jesus Christ instructed in the Bible. The moment I made that decision and did what the Bible says must be done to receive God's invitation into His household, God became my Father in Heaven. He sent His Spirit to live in me to help me, comfort me, teach me, and show me things that I could not come up with on my own. So, whenever I do projects like this one I ask the Holy Spirit for help. He brings to my remembrance things from long ago that I had forgotten about. He helps me determine the difference between fantasies that have nothing to do with what I was born to do and dreams that truly are a key to my life's calling. He also gives me direction and instruction on unlocking the talents that I have been given by God. If you have not been introduced to the loving King, Jesus Christ, Who gave His own life for you, I suggest you look into doing that very soon. You will find that He loves you very much and is eagerly waiting to help you live a powerful, happy and successful life.

I am not one to pressure someone into something they do not want or are not ready for, so I leave it up to you to pursue this important issue. However, I am going to make it as easy for you as I can. You do not even have to get up from where you are sitting, or log onto some website. If you are interested, just turn to page 83.

The Second Way:

Enhance the Splendor of Your Surroundings with Lights -
Focusing on you and your neighbors

    This project takes from an already existing tradition and embellishes it. It is a tradition that adds splendor and awestruck gasps to the atmosphere. It is the adorning of house, yard, trees, buildings and whatever you desire with lights. Lights can turn a boring tree into a shining object of beauty. They can outline pleasant angles on boxy structures. Color and illumination bring life to cold hard forms. Like the glow of a fire, pretty lights can almost draw people into a trance of awe and wonder. Twinkling, trailing, intermittent blinking, flashing in patterns, lights even bring movement and rhythm to their supporting framework. In recent years, lights have been creatively woven together and packaged in such a way that they look similar to lace hanging from the edges of the roof when properly installed.

    This is a way that you can use to bring delight to your neighbors around you. Not only will you be brightening your yard while adding to the festive atmosphere of the neighborhood, but your neighbor will have the pleasure of seeing your seasonal decorations from their own next door perspective. The concept of having close-knit neighbors was widely accepted and practiced back when people needed the help of those who lived near by to build a barn or recover strayed livestock or borrow a horse for transport. However, since folks have become more independent and busy they do not see the need for developing a friendship with those to whom they live in close proximity. They are missing out on something wonderful that enhances daily life.

    Picture yourself pulling out of your driveway on the way to work. You see your neighbor in his driveway picking up a recently delivered newspaper. He stands up and notices you giving you a polite nod of the head and partial wave of the hand just to be courteous. There is no kind sharing of thoughts of friendship only vague ponderings of what each other might be thinking of the other. What if instead, when you see him he stands up and notices you and warmly smiles while waving good bye? As his friend you return a warm smile and wave and your mood is more cheerful now having shared a pleasant moment with a good friend; someone you have gotten to know, to trust and to appreciate over time.

Close neighbors make for frequent encounters.
Make the most of them.

Surprise your neighbor with a tin of fresh-baked cookies.

Think of those days when you come home weary from work. Those times when you feel just brushed aside or walked on by people who do not even realize how they affected you. You pull into the driveway trying to clear your mind of the day's events that seem like such a blur at this point. Your favorite chair sits with open arms beckoning you to plop in and close your eyes giving way to a deep sigh. Upon opening your eyes you see through your window a neighbor out working in the back yard. Do you see just another self-absorbed, distant person or does your countenance lift a little as you view that neighbor as a friend? Is there a certain comfort in knowing that they are there when you need a little something like a few eggs, a specific tool or just an extra set of hands for a small project? It works the other way as well. Lonely and tired your neighbor may just need the assurance from having met you that you are a kind soul who is there for them. You are not some rude non-caring scrooge.

Maybe you are one of those neighbors who have been too busy to take the first step to get to know your next door neighbors. Make this year be the year that you enhance your own life and the lives of those around you by being friendly. Take them a box of lights as a gift. Use the opportunity to introduce yourself and offer your help in areas in which you would feel comfortable helping them. Do it early in the season so that they can have their box of lights in plenty of time to string them up any way they want. Because people get so busy going to holiday parties and visiting relatives and all, it is difficult to catch them at home. So when you start early in trying to contact them you have time to retry failed earlier attempts.

Now it is time to go home and start on your own house. Putting the lights on the tree, garlands, wreaths and other needled decorations is best done before any other trim is added. So before your unroll the ribbon, before you unpack the ornaments, before you break out the hand-crafted keep-sakes, be sure all your lights work and are in place. Keep safety in mind when using extension cords and various outlets. Check labels for ability to use the lights indoors and outdoors.

Look through magazines and books to get some fresh ideas. Be creative in your approach to accenting an object. In southern states light displays on the ground are popular, especially along driveways and flowerbeds. The deep snow across the northern states hampers this particular canvas from being visible for much of the season.

Purchase a couple partitions and carefully cover them with strings of lights. Make sure the lights are evenly distributed so the partitions keep their balance. Then set the partitions up to form a tunnel walkway just inside your front door.

How many is too many lights?
Which one makes them twinkle?

A light-covered partition can also be used as an unusual back drop for your project from Way One of this book, or it could serve as a fun temporary wall for the season. Add pizzazz to your Christmas tree by placing one light-covered partition on either side. This would help to extend the gift placement area by highlighting any large presents that do not fit under the tree if gift-giving is a part of your holiday tradition.

Transform select doorways in your house into glistening portals of entry by affixing strings of lights in the form of curtains draping down and drawn back with rich ribbon and tassel tie-backs.

Try weaving a string of lights through an artificial centerpiece on your dining room table. DO NOT put lights in an arrangement in which there is water. Leave some slack in the cord so that it can be gently secured to the underside of the table, along a table leg and across the floor to the outlet without tripping anyone or catching on someone's leg, pulling the whole centerpiece onto the floor. It's a bummer when that happens.

For those looking for something out of the norm and are willing to put a little elbow grease into it, this suggestion applies to those who have tall clumps of ornamental grass such as Pampas Grass or Fountain Grass. At the end of the fall season after the grass has lost its green color, leave it tall so that you can separate the grass clump in handful size bundles still attached to the clump. Be sure to drive a slender, tall yet sturdy, stake right next to the clump for each bundle to be formed around. Only the outer edges of the clump of grass need to be formed into bundles. It is not necessary to disturb the center of the clump. For a more decorative, smoother look, each bundle could be braided around its stake. This braiding takes a lot of work, but if this intrigues you the step by step process is explained on page 26.

    In the above picture the grass was braided when it was still green in color, showing signs of continued growth. Coincidently, the grass compensated for the cutting off of light from the blades that had been braided together, by growing all new blades around the braids swallowing them up in a sea of new grass. If the grass is braided after signs of growth are gone and the grass is at rest for the winter then the braids should remain visible, free from being encased by replacement blades.

    Either procedure used on the tall grass calls for the person doing the bundling (or braiding) to wear long pants, long sleeves, and gloves if possible. If proper clothing is not worn be prepared for several small cuts similar to paper cuts.

    After all bundles are tightly tied around their own stake, wrap each bundle (or braid) with outdoor lights like you would the trunk of a small tree. Try to use newer lights whose cords are not worn and be sure the lights are labeled for outdoor use. Avoiding fire hazards is important so wrap the points of connection between cords with a nonflammable material.

For those interested in braiding their ornamental grass:

1. Begin by grabbing a handful of grass and separating it from the rest of the clump by loosely wrapping surrounding intrusive grass with a long thin wire or a string. Then start at ground level and separate the handful of grass into three equal sections.
2. Smooth out the sections with your fingers making all blades of grass go in the same direction parallel to each other as you pull them upward into a straight standing-up position keeping a stake in the center of the braid.
3. Carefully crisscross the sections of grass into a braid (around the stake). Tie off the top of the braid with a piece or string or twine that will match nicely with the grass.
4. Now you are ready to wrap each braid in lights. Remember to unwrap the intrusive grass that you corralled with wire or string in step 1.

Here is another time when I, as a believer in God, rely on the Holy Spirit to give me unusual ideas, witty new inventions and even the right words to say to my neighbor. Remember, I am not going to annoy you with constant badgering but if you are curious, desiring to know more about this spiritual helper I direct you to page 83.

The Third Way:

Reach Out to the Ones
That Tug on Your Heart –
Focusing on those less fortunate

    This project will quickly become a favorite for each family member. It involves setting aside some time to focus on someone else. First determine a group of people or even animals that have an effect on your heart. For example, when you visit a nursing home and see the elderly sitting alone, some deserted by family members and others empty of love, does it just pull at your heart? When you see children that are less fortunate than others maybe because of being in a low-income family or maybe there is a learning disorder to deal with, does that stir some desire in you to help in some way? If you have walked into an animal shelter and sensed that more needed to be done for these precious little lives cut off from the outdoors, then maybe they are your target group. Some families volunteer together as a team helping out in their local soup kitchen feeding the homeless. It could be that you saw a story about the millions of Chinese baby girls that are discarded, rescued by orphanages that are already full but cannot bear to let these helpless ones die in the streets; and you told yourself that when you were more able that you would send help to them somehow. Well, there is never going to be that "perfect time" to help so you just have to do what you can with what you currently have.
    Determining to do this every year gives you the reason and opportunity to do something to reach out to that group of lives that have caught the attention of your soul. Visit the place where the group resides to gather information on their biggest need. If visiting in person is not possible, then contact them online or by phone. Communicate with them in some way to find out how you could make the biggest impact for their good. Some may suggest giving money for supplies and medical care.

Others may suggest giving food. A hand made card or present filled with words of encouragement and love sometimes makes a lasting impression. Even something as simple as making the time to listening to an older person's story or consulting with a child's parents for some playtime with you or cuddling an old dog outside of his cold wire cage could be the life-changing goal of this holiday project. If your visit is in person, be sure to take your camera and ask someone if it would be alright to take pictures of you with your new found friend. These will serve as items of memorabilia for you and for your new friend as well as visuals for those with whom you share the joys of your encounter.

It is this project that actually portrays the heart of Jesus Christ. His life was spent bringing hope and healing to those that were hurting and discarded by society. It draws us to love through actually doing something not just saying nice words. The Holy Spirit inside a child of God can actually strengthen the love in that person's heart so that patience and kindness can continue to be strong in them even if their efforts to love are rejected or unappreciated. Like some of these less fortunate creatures that we reach out to, we had no idea that Jesus was reaching out to us, loving us while we were still in a not very lovable state. He loved us before we even thought about whether to love Him or not.

Mmmmhhhhmmmm. No pressure so I am not going to say it, but you know what I am thinking. Page 83.

Siblings cuddling siblings.

Best friends imparting affection to precious creatures, together.

Do not underestimate the value of a visit.

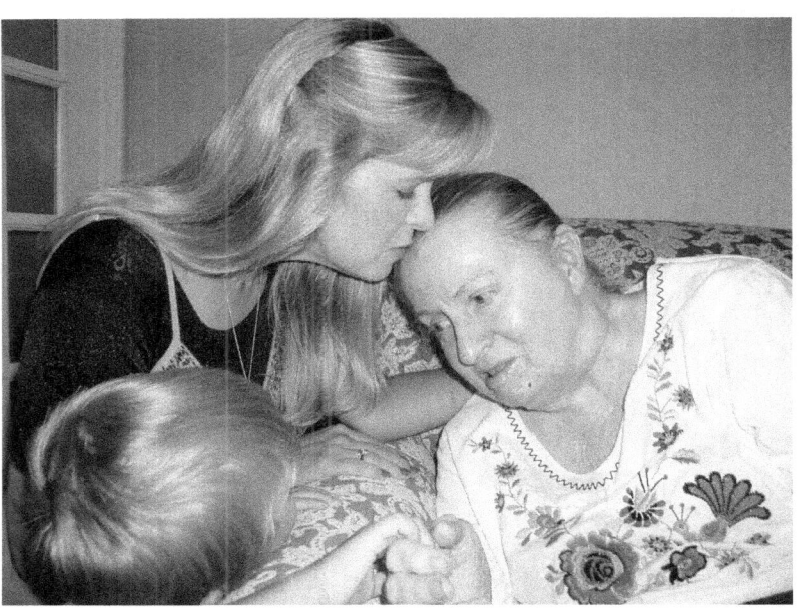

Good memories in the making.

What is it like going from a cold wire cage to warm loving arms? Help some animals find out the answer this year.

The Fourth Way:

Compile Calendars and Create Crafts –
Focusing on extended family, friends and children

A Christmas, no matter how wonderful would not be as meaningful without family and close friends. The tradition of gathering together, traveling long distances and setting aside time to be together should always be a part of the Christmas holiday. This fourth project centers on bonding time with family and friends. Each member of the family gets to hunt for a gift for themselves. It is a specific gift that fits their precise need and reflects their personality and even dreams. Because it is something that they will see every day of the year and possibly have visible in their home or work, they should be the one to choose its appearance and functionality. Have you guessed what it is? - a calendar. Some people prefer small desk-top calendars, others large picturesque calendars while even others demand a calendar consisting of daily removable pages that provide room for written notes. Additional supplies to accompany this project are sticky notes or some type of small note papers to be attached to others calendars, and pens to be passed out throughout the visit. More fun activities for children are mentioned later in this section.

When it is time to gather together each member must bring their calendar to each gathering. Each person writes one important date on each sticky note, either at the visit or ahead of time. Write the importance such as birthday along with any desired details such as which birthday it will be this year. Some examples are: March 12th -Tami turns 16; or June 14th -Mary & Jon's 5th Anniversary; May (exact day may not be known yet)- Sue graduates this year; October 10th- Anne's baby is due. Get a count of how many members are at the gathering and then write the same important date on that number of sticky notes. If there are 12 people present with their calendars then write the special date and details on twelve separate sticky notes. Depending on what works best either have all the calendars set out together or pass them around among the group.

Attach each sticky note to each corresponding month on each calendar. An example for Tami would be to attach one of her sticky notes about her birthday on the month of March of every calendar. Mary or Jon would secure one of their sticky notes of their anniversary on the month of June of every calendar. By the time members begin to part for other destinations their calendar should be filled with sticky notes on each month in which there is a date that is special to another member that is at that gathering. The reason the sticky notes are used is so that the owner of the calendar may go home and arrange and record the dates the way that is most helpful and legible to them. Sometimes people's penmanship makes it difficult to determine the needed information. If this is the case either kindly inquire of the author of the note to clarify what is written, or ask a close relative to help you interpret the unique style of writing.

Another approach to accomplishing this project would be for each person to type and print out all their special occasions with dates ahead of time on one page with their name on it. Be sure to make enough copies to put one copy on the calendar of every person that is involved in the get-togethers. With this method it may be helpful to accompany each calendar with a folder for the papers gathered. Each person then should keep the left-over copies of their own special dates with them as they go from gathering to gathering to distribute at each opportunity. This eliminates the problem of illegible hand writing and loose masses of Post-It notes.

Since most of the family and friends are together conveniently in one or two places this would be the perfect time to gather and confirm fun facts about each other. On page 39 is a suggested set of questions. Other questions can be used but be sure to consider the participants to make sure you do not ask questions to which they do not mind other people knowing the answers. Make plenty of copies incase some of the relatives would like to have fun trying to guess the answers to the questions for another person. Each person should supply the real answers on a copy of their own. This could be done every other year or so since answers to the questions could change from year to year.

Note that a positive atmosphere fosters better memories. Do your best to discourage family gatherings from turning into complaints sessions. Whether the topic gravitates toward an over-bearing boss, a dead-end job or even a hum-drum life in general encourage thoughts of thankfulness and humor. Always look on the good side of things. Maybe change the subject to a fun movie you have seen this year or a comical incident that happened involving your pet (if you have one).

Some medical researches have shown laughter to be healthy for the body. The Bible agrees with this finding and instructs people to think on only positive things. Proverbs 17:22 reads, "A cheerful heart is good medicine, but a crushed spirit dries up the bones." (See page 89 for another Bible verse that supports this claim.)

Smiles are contagious and tend to resurface when brought back in remembrance even years later.

The closer the friends, the stronger the trust, - and the more opportunities to have fun being silly.

1) What is your favorite movie?
2) What is your favorite restaurant?
3) What is your favorite store in which to shop?
4) What is your favorite entrée: steak, shrimp, seafood, chicken, sushi, ribs, pork, lasagna, spaghetti, pizza, tacos, fajitas, tamales, salads, home cooking?
5) What is your favorite desert?
6) Which would you prefer: coffee or tea? What would you order if going to Starbucks?
7) Would you rather snow ski or stroll on a warm beach?
8) In the whole world, where would you most like to go on vacation?
9) What kind of music do you like to listen to most?
10) Would you rather work on a hobby or read a book?
11) What is your favorite show on television?
12) When you have spare time, what is your favorite thing to do?
13) If you could have any animal in the world knowing it had been trained to use a litter box, not bite or injure in any way, nor destroy furniture etc., what animal would you want for a pet?
14) What would you consider to be the perfect job for you?
15) Do large groups of people drain you or energize you?
16) Who was the last person to whom you sent a text message?
17) Which of your memories do you feel is the funniest?
18) What place were you visiting when you were farthest from home?
19) If you could change your first name, what would you change it to?
20) What is your love language- What means most to you –
Hugs, holding hands and maybe cuddling on the couch;
Little Notes of kindness;
Gifts for no other reason than to say "I love you";
Acts of Kindness (someone doing chores for you to lesson your load);
or Quality Time spent with just you and your loved one?

After all gatherings are over and each member is comfortably safe at home, they each can unpack their personal calendar. It should be chock full of sticky notes gathered from all the friends and family members that they had visited; or paired with a folder full of papers containing all the special dates. This is where the project can become a work of art. Jump into it with a wildly creative flare. Try setting up a code for birthdays, anniversaries, graduations, weddings, births, and other special occasions. Various colors of small stickers could be used to represent a category. Our corresponding example could be a blue sticker on March 12th accompanied by Tami's name and the number 16 written on the sticker showing that Tami turns 16 on this day. Adhesive rhinestones, foam shapes, letters and numbers along with ink stamps and other small marking devices can be found at your local hobby store or online.

Armed with all the special dates that were collected the owner of each calendar now has the opportunity to reconnect with the author of each note on their special day with a card, a gift, a phone call, an email, or whatever they choose. This provides a way to give gifts at a manageable, reasonable pace accompanied by much thought, preparation, and budgeting.

If each family member and friend would be diligent to do this throughout the year, having been kept up to date on all the special names and dates then quite possibly when that time of year comes around for everyone to gather again for Christmas the exchanging of presents may become less of a focus and priority. The burden of anxious shopping, commercialization, and the stress of trying to appease each other, outdo each other or even just satisfy each other should become less of a part of this joyful time of year.

The expense of flight tickets, or gas, groceries, or party trays, would be best spent in hopes of coming together to show how much each member means to one another. It is always a good idea to let the ones you love know how much you cherish them. Showing interest in what has happened in the last year in their lives and even asking them about their goals and plans for the coming year is a good way to gather hints for gifts to give them on their special days ahead.

What about the children? How boring are calendars and chat sessions for two through twelve year olds? Well, this would be a good time to group them all around the same area that has been lined with a drop cloth or made safe some how for the furniture and let them assemble simple crafts together. Having constructed the crafts around the same table with their cousins and friends the craft can become an item of memorabilia that each child can cherish in the years ahead and even take to school for show and tell. Implore each family ahead of time to bring one or more supplies for the craft time.

To make things easier, here is a suggested list of items:

- Crayons or markers
- Children's scissors
- Glue
- Clothes pins
- Tissue paper cut in squares and possibly crinkled
- Chenille stems/pipe-cleaners/bendable fuzzy wires
- Cotton balls
- Construction paper and foam sheets
- Foam shapes
- Stickers
- Yarn – various colors
- Glitter or glitter glue
- Toothpicks
- Styrofoam balls – different sizes
- Beads and string – various colors
- Felt rectangles – various colors
- Tooth picks
- Sunflower seeds
- Sequins – various colors
- Rhinestone gems – various colors
- Small buttons – various colors
- Drinking straws – normal sized

Have the supplies wrapped as separate presents for the whole group to share. Get the kids excited about what materials they have to work with. You could have them draw numbers that correspond to one of the wrapped set of supplies. Then have each child unwrap the present whose number they drew. Each child gets to open an equal number of presents housing surprise materials. Supervising adults open any excess supplies with enthusiasm.

You may choose any items that the group feels the children would enjoy and be safe working with. It may be that all the families agree to ask the crafty one of the group to gather all the supplies while everyone else pitch in to help with the cost.

Here are five different simple craft suggestions using some of the items listed on page 42.

Snowman

1) Connect three Styrofoam balls with toothpicks by sliding one small ball on one end of the toothpick; then slide a medium sized ball on the other end of the tooth pick. Then stick a second toothpick into the center of the medium ball next to the other toothpick and slide the large ball on the end of the second toothpick that is sticking out. You should now have three Styrofoam balls joined together in a row, having the large ball on the bottom and small ball on top. If the balls seem to be loose on the toothpicks, then remove the toothpicks and fill the holes with glue and reinsert the toothpicks where they belong.
2) Have an adult carefully slice the rounded end off the bottom of the large ball with a knife making the three ball structure stand flat, straight, and sturdy.
3) Now you may choose to glue a thin layer of cotton all over the three balls or just leave them as is. Next select two Sunflower seeds and poke them into the small ball to represent eyes. Pull them back out and insert glue into the holes made by the seeds then poke the seeds back into the glue-filled holes.
4) Glue a large sequin, bead, or small button on for the nose.
5) Glue an upward-curved line of rhinestones or sequins onto the small ball just under the nose to represent its mouth. You make choose to just make an upward-curved line on the ball with glitter glue to form the mouth, nose or eyes.

6) Cut about three pieces of yarn approximately four inches long to wrap around its neck as a scarf. If you choose to braid the yarn start with a knot on one end, braid the yarn, then finish with a knot on the other end. The scarf could also just be made out of a strip of felt cut from a felt square.
7) Insert toothpicks or two to three inch pieces of chenille stems into the medium ball to represent arms. If you choose to use the chenille stems make the hole in the medium ball first with a toothpick, then remove the toothpick, insert glue then insert the chenille stems. The chenille stems arms can be bent at any desired position.
8) Cut four small glove shapes out of foam or construction paper, then glue two of the gloves together with the tip of an arm sandwiched in between. Glue the other two sandwiched around the tip of the other arm.

Stable or House

1) Fold one piece of construction paper into equal thirds, then lay flat again. The middle section between the two folds will be the roof of the building, the outer two sections will form the front and back of the building.
2) Draw, decorate and color any desired windows, doors, people, animals, etc.. on the front and back sections on the top side of the paper. You may choose to use crayons, markers, glitter glue, stickers, cotton balls, rhinestones, foam shapes, whatever.
3) Now gather four drinking straws. Make four one-half inch slits straight down and at equal distances apart from each other on one end of each of the four straws. Press the straw open so at the slits so that it forms four arms straight out from the straw at right angles to the straw.
4) Repeat step three on the opposite end of each straw only using one inch slits, forming one inch arms

coming out, having been pressed open at right angles from the straw.
5) Cut four three inch squares out of foam sheets. Foam does not slip around like paper does.
6) Glue or secure the four foam squares to the end of each straw that has the one inch arms sticking out. The arms make it easier to secure the straw so that it stands straight up.
7) Fold the paper from step one, which is now decorated, at the two folds.
8) Glue or secure the end of each of the four straws that has the one-half inch arms radiating out to the four corners of the underside of the roof part of the folded paper. You should end up with a folded piece of paper glued on top of four straws that are standing straight up kept from slipping by foam pieces under each straw. The front and back sections of the decorated paper should cover the top half of the straws. Little figurines or dolls can be placed under the building.

Christmas Card Stands

1) Cut paper into three and a half to four inch squares.
2) Draw, color, and decorate pictures on the squares of paper as desired using whatever materials desired such as glitter glue, sequins, seeds, cotton balls, markers, foam shapes, pieces of yarn, crinkled tissue paper, etc..
3) Glue the decorated papers to the flat side of a clothespin, front or back or both, making sure that the bottom of the picture that is on the square is on the bottom of the clothespin that you pinch to open the clothespin. So when you open the clothespin you will be touching the bottom of the picture. The top of the picture should be at the top of the clothespin that clips to the Christmas card.

4) Clip one clothespin to each of the two bottom corners of your favorite Christmas card that you have received and stand it up. You should have a Christmas card being held up by two or more clothespins hidden by decorated squares.

Ornament Hanger

1) Form a circle using the bottom four inches of chenille stem (preferably gold or silver) leaving the remainder of the chenille stem sticking straight up and slightly arched outward away from the circle.
2) Bend the top two inches of the chenille stem forward over the circle and down then bend the tip up to form a hook on which to hang light weight ornaments.
3) Decorate three to four inch circles of paper like ornaments. You may choose to decorate small Styrofoam balls. Keep in mind they must remain light in weight. The chenille stems will not be able to hold heavy objects.
4) Glue or tape a two inch string/yarn to the top of the decorated paper forming a loop with which to hang it.
5) If hanging a Styrofoam ball attach the string/yarn by lining the two ends of the string/yarn up alongside each other and tying a knot close to the ends. This will form a loop in the remaining string/yarn. Then insert a toothpick through the middle of the knot with half to three fourths of the toothpick sticking out under the knot. Now poke a hole in the top of the Styrofoam ball with the toothpick. Remove the toothpick from the hole and fill the hole with glue. Once again insert the toothpick into the hole making sure that it is still poking through the knot in the string/yarn. Push the toothpick all the way into the ball until it reaches the knot of string/yarn that is three fourths the way up the toothpick. Press the knot into any glue that has gushed out of the hole next to the toothpick. If no excess glue has come out of the hole, then put some glue on the ball right at the base of the

toothpick where it comes out of the hole and press the knot into the glue so that it does not slip up the fourth of the toothpick that is still sticking up out of the knot and ball.

Personalized Mini Tapestry

1) First cut a piece of string or yarn approximately twenty-four inches long to use for hanging the banner, and set aside.
2) Then select the color of felt rectangle you desire for the main background of the banner.
3) Fold the felt rectangle in half leaving you with a long thin rectangle. Folding it precisely in equal halves will ensure that your tapestry comes to a point centered exactly in the middle of the bottom edge. Start at the tip of the folded edge at the bottom of your piece of felt and trim a wedge angled diagonally toward the sides of the rectangle to about four inches up from the bottom edge. This should leave your tapestry with a point shape at the bottom from which you may choose to hang a small tassel or jingle bell.
4) Turn the felt over to the backside and mark a line across the top two inches down from the top edge. Make the mark straight from one side all the way to the other.
5) Put glue across the backside top edge – just the edge, not the whole two inches below, and fold backward to the line that you marked two inches down from that top edge. Press the top edge down and smooth it all the way across. You should end up with a sleeve/tunnel at the top of your piece of felt.
6) Decorate the banner any way you desire. Some may want their tapestry to display their name or a cheerful greeting, while others may want it to display a snowman or winter scene. Encourage creativity using glitter glue, sequins, rhinestone gems, beads, buttons, pieces of yarn, cotton balls, other pieces of felt, etc. A

decorative edging can even be glued on such as rick-rack, lace, ribbon, or jingle bells. (Parents you even may choose to sew or glue a shape onto the felt ahead of time for the children to decorate.)

7) Now get a normal sized drinking straw and feed it through the tunnel/sleeve you made in the top of the felt tapestry.

8) Next feed the yarn or string through the straw. If having trouble getting it through the straw tie a toothpick as close to the end of the string as possible and lower it through the straw, then untie the toothpick once outside the other end of the straw.

9) Now with one end of the string or yarn coming out one end of the straw and the other end of the string or yarn coming out the other end of the straw tie the two ends of the string or yarn together tightly into a knot. Pull the string or yarn until the knot is hidden inside the middle of the straw.

If there are several older children and teens in the group then maybe a more involved craft could be constructed like a model airplane or model car for each teen. What about supplying each young person with a plain pillow case or plain T-shirt, having them put their name on it, then having all the young people pass them around for each one to sign? If no creativity at all is desired then good board games or card games can be fun. If apathy and lame attitudes surface then give incentive such as announcing that all game participants receive a numbered ticket for the opportunity to win a really cool door prize. Having prepared before-hand for such an occasion, pass out numbered pieces of paper to each one that participates in the games available. When the first young person has to leave then reach into a bowl of papers with corresponding numbers (also prepared before-hand) and randomly select one. Try to make the prize worth their while for participating.

God designed the family unit which was to include healthy family relationships. He Himself requested that His people all journey to Jerusalem once a year as a family. The idea was to bring a thank gift to God and have fun in gratitude for all He had done for them throughout that past year. There was eating together, dancing with joy before God, thanking God, enjoying time in God's presence and just enjoying each other in an atmosphere of thankfulness and love. We can do that once a year at Christmas.

Gifts to God and His kingdom through orphanages, ministries that have made an impact on you, or organizations that help the needy such as the Salvation Army would make a commendable family tradition as well. By the way, just in case you may have an extra few minutes to check out what an author like me would be so excited about, page 83 should still be there waiting for you to peruse at your own leisurely pace.

Do the gifts for each relative have to be given all at one time of the year? It can be such a burden for some.

Good memories last longer than most gifts and are a lot easier to make.

The Fifth Way:

Honor Saint Nicholas Properly And Restore the Innocence of the Spirit of the Season –
Focusing on children
and those who influence them

This last way has everything to do with the children. So many parents enjoy the evidence of true innocence in their children during the Christmas season when people all around them begin to talk about Santa Claus. Do you encourage your children to believe in Santa Claus? Do you desire to exercise their imagination and teach them to dream? Maybe you do not even have children but you just want to spread holiday cheer through bringing joy and hope to people of all ages by pretending that Santa Claus is real. You mean well, only having good intentions in your heart.

I remember as a child the sight of this jolly magical man ignited a whole dream world inside my heart. Awakening the stories of flying reindeer, little hardworking elves, the fortress at the North Pole and most of all, the generous over-weight man in the red suit who brings whatever gift you ask for, sparked a renewed sense of adventure for me. I dove into the season as if it were a totally different dimension of existence. To me it was a dimension where a happy man checked to see if I had been bad or good then sought to visit malls and other appointed places to patiently listen the request of each and every boy and girl standing in line to sit on his lap. It almost unleashed within me a sense of greed. It was a time when it seemed ok to ask for the one thing I really wanted without feeling selfish because I knew the other kids would get what they wanted too. This dimension housed these things that do not happen in the dimension of the rest of the year.

Children having impressionable, hungry minds, like mine was, drink in readily the options given them as an alternative to a stagnant or unsatisfied life. This is why it is so important to be the good influence in their lives. They should be told that Saint Nicholas was a man who deserves recognition as a man who lived like Jesus had instructed each of us to live.

http://en.wikipedia.org/wiki/Saint_Nicholas gives an account of the origin of Saint Nicholas. It states, "**Saint Nicholas** (Greek: Ἅγιος Νικόλαος , *Agios Nikolaos*, "victory of the people") (270 - 6 December 346) is the common name for **Nicholas of Myra**, a saint and Bishop of Myra (in Lycia, part of modern-day Turkey). Because of the many miracles attributed to his intercession, he is also known as **Nicholas the Wonderworker**. He had a reputation for secret gift-giving, such as putting coins in the shoes of those who left them out for him, and thus became the model for Santa Claus, whose English name comes from the German **Sankt Niklaus**. His reputation evolved among the faithful, as is common for early Christian saints.[2] In 1087, his relics were furtively translated to Bari, in southern Italy; for this reason, he is also known as **Nicholas of Bari**."

http://www.stnicholascenter.org/Brix?pageID=40 also provides stories behind who Saint Nicholas really was. It states, "As Bishop of Myra, Nicholas lived the qualities that caused his fame and popularity to spread throughout the Christian world. His vigorous actions on behalf of his people and in defense of the Christian faith reveal a man who lived his convictions. Nicholas was not timid—he did what was necessary and was not easily intimidated by others' power and position. His concern for the welfare of his flock and his stand for orthodox belief earned him respect as a model for bishops and a defender of the faith." It summarizes, "As a bishop, Nicholas, servant of God, was first and foremost a shepherd of the people, caring for their needs. His active pursuit of justice for his people was demonstrated when he secured grain in time of famine, saved the lives of three men wrongly condemned, and secured lower taxes for Myra. He taught the Gospel simply, so ordinary people understood, and he lived out his faith and devotion to God in helping the poor and all in need."

The real Saint Nicholas was humble and generous. It was his obedience to Jesus' teachings that made him turn out to be the honorable man that he was. God was able to do powerful miracles through him. We would do good to honor Saint Nicholas's memory in an appropriate way just like we do for Abraham Lincoln, George Washington and Dr. Martin Luther King. This was done for many years, however, somewhere in history there was introduced a new slant to Saint Nicholas's profile. The fictional character of Santa Claus began to take shape. It was more of a magical figure than the original human Saint Nicholas.

What was for generations a sweet little story that added just a touch of fairy-tale fun to the season has now developed into much more than that. People get angry when the topic of removing Santa from Christmas comes up because it does not seem that harmful, but instead it appears to actually interject good back into the cold busy world around us. Yet they need to stop and observe just what this fairy tale has grown to become, especially to children who are not allowed to celebrate what their family believes in public but are instead encouraged to acknowledge Santa Claus.

Some claim that keeping the idea of the magical Santa Claus alive keeps the child's innocence in tact. They feel that removing this magical Santa Claus from the Holiday Season would remove children's innocence as well.

One such person on the internet put it this way in his article entitled: "Let Santa Live as Long as Possible, Too Many Parents Ruin Santa for Their Children, Why?" "There really is nothing quite like watching the face of a child light up as they write Santa a letter or the joy a child gets sitting on Santa's lap. The innocence of a child is a big part of what makes time of the year so special. Yet too many parents feel the need to ruin this innocence by disclosing the truth about Santa's 'origins' to their kids."
(www.associatedcontent.com/pop_print.shtml?content_type)

By this manner of thinking some conclude that the discovery of the truth corrupts innocence. The reality of it is that the children are vulnerable to trust what people tell them. Innocence carries in it a lack of pride; a lack of believing that you know more than your parents. It is full of hope in things that are beyond laws of science and realms of possibilities. So with truth comes knowledge that empowers the children to start to reason out impossibilities. This causes their dreams to begin to set limits as to what can really happen. Therefore, the people that feel truth corrupts would conclude that if truth is withheld and replaced by fun characters which do things that are not normally possible then the children's dreams and hopes will continue without limit and without reason.

The true removal of innocence happens when the vulnerable state of a child's mind is fed a story that will one day be found to have been untrue. If the vulnerable mind of the child were fed with truth about a being who really does exist, whose power is limitless and who loves them deeply, then there would never come a day when what was believed in would be found to be false. There would only continue to be discovery of more truth which then would only lead to continued innocence. There would be less of a sense of the pride that leads to resistance of trust in what was told them. Since no lie had ever really been introduced to them, by those that taught them (whom they had learned to trust), they would not feel the need to search reality for themselves to see if it was really true or not. Furthermore, their dreams would only get more extensive in scope as they uncover more ways in which this being can communicate with them and work in them. This being, of course, would be Jesus Christ, Son of the one real God, God Almighty, God of Abraham, Isaac and Jacob.

No, my intention is not to pressure you into believing. However, let me ask you this; if you discovered the cure for horrible debilitating diseases such as cancer, Alzheimer's, Parkinson's Disease, and so many others would you not be bursting to tell everyone you knew so that they could get cured or at least find hope and peace in the middle of the affliction? Or if you knew that people were headed for a terrible disaster and you found the only way for them to turn to safety, would you just stay silent watching them all unknowingly walk right into danger? That is how I feel about telling people of the One whom I truly believe is the answer to all we face, and the One who reigns over all eternity.

If you do not believe in God is it because you too have lost your innocence? What are the reasons you would not accept the idea of a God Who is limitless in power, Who loves you, and Who has only good intentions toward you? Is it because you learned as a child that those who told you of things like God were also the ones who told you about Santa Claus? You might have deducted from that experience that you had learned not to be so gullible. This is one example of why leading children to believe in the magical story of Santa Claus can be damaging to them. The choking of the faith in a child's heart is the result of this widely accepted holiday tradition.

This is not an attempt to tell or encourage anyone to hate Santa Claus. God is love, not hate. He tells us to love one another, and that is the motive behind this book. Because of love for parents, children and people of all ages, this truth is being shared to help them all see the truth and make a change to get them back to spiritual and physical safety and to a position where they can have a better relationship with God Almighty.
God included in His book, the Bible, this request in the section entitled Romans 12:18, 21:
"If possible, so far as it depends on you, live peaceably with all…Do not be overcome by evil, but overcome evil with good." (English Standard Version)

The same individual from the internet that I had mentioned earlier explained Santa this way: "Santa is no different than the Christmas Spirit or the magic of the Season. Santa is the feeling that comes from listening to your favorite Christmas songs or being charitable during the holidays. Santa is the calm feeling we get as we lay our heads down on Christmas Eve knowing that presents will be under the tree upon our awakening."
(www.associatedcontent.com/pop_print.shtml?content_type)

All these things he mentioned (Christmas Spirit, magic of the Season, feelings of joy, and inclinations to give) have nothing to do with some fictional character, and can still exist in powerful ways in the absence of Santa Claus. These feelings and inner promptings to do good deeds are stemming from the spirit within each of us and are intensified when Jesus is welcomed to exist in your heart.

There really is a whole realm that humans are a part of that they cannot see nor pin point with science. There is evidence of it in many things that science cannot explain. It is the realm of the spirit. God is spirit and He made humans to be part physical body but also part spirit. These distinctively different parts are intricately intertwined with each other. The two are only separated at specific times such as when the physical body dies. It is the spirit that rises up to continue to exist while the physical body begins to decay. Incidentally, it is the spirit in a person that gives life to their body. If a person's spirit is weak and small because of depression, fear or even anger, then it can actually drain life from the physical body. Conversely, if a person's spirit is thriving, growing stronger because of focusing on God's positive words then it will bring life into the physical body. The Biblical book of Proverbs 18:14 reads, "A man's spirit sustains him in sickness, but a crushed spirit who can bear?"

All things that have to do with God are based on spirit activity. There are spiritual laws that govern the spiritual realm just like there are physical laws, such as the Law of Gravity, or the Laws of Physics, that govern the physical realm. These laws are boundary lines that people must learn to be aware of and handle properly.

If a father told his son not to stick a fork into the light socket on the wall next to him, then the father had to leave the room for a minute, what would happen to the son if he decided to do what he felt like and stick the fork in the socket instead of taking the instruction of his father? Would the laws of physics that govern electricity shut down for a minute and be all of a sudden unreliable just because of the ignorance of the boy? No, the laws of physics would prove true without respect to who was testing them. The boy's injury would not come from the father punishing him, but instead from the electricity that the father had warned the boy not to go near. The wise father knowing the laws of electricity and having loved the son had given instruction to keep the son safe.

So it is with God, Who knows the Laws of the Spiritual realm very well, Who gives us instruction to keep us safe because He loves us so much. Yet it is God that people blame many times when those dependable spiritual laws do what they do because that is how those spiritual laws work. Many people do not recognize the spiritual side of things resulting in a misunderstanding of how the physical and spiritual elements interact, and thus a misinterpretation of the cause and effect. This is why so many people do not see the harm in coaxing children to believe in Santa Claus during the Christmas season.

Good intentioned relatives and friends, with the help of media and movies, foster the start of a relationship between their children and this imaginary character. The efforts to do this have developed in recent years, especially in movies and media to where it has become a very elaborate, well-planned out ordeal. It did not use to be so pronounced when I was a child. This website http://en.wikipedia.org/wiki/Santa_Claus, even states:

"Some people have created websites designed to allow children and other interested parties to "track" Santa Claus on Christmas Eve via radar; while in transit, Santa Claus is sometimes escorted by Canadian Air Force fighter jets.[37]

In 1955, a Sears Roebuck store in Colorado Springs, Colorado, gave children a number to call a "Santa hotline". The number was mistyped and children called the Continental Air Defense Command (CONAD) on Christmas Eve instead. The Director of Operations, Col. Harry Shoup, received the first call for Santa and responded by telling children that there were signs on the radar that Santa was indeed heading south from North Pole. In 1958, Canada and the United States jointly created the North American Air Defense Command (NORAD) and together tracked Santa Claus for children of North America that year and ever since.[38] This tracking can now be done by children via the

Internet and NORAD's website. Many local television stations in the United States and Canada likewise track Santa Claus in their own metropolitan areas through the stations' meteorologists.

Many other websites are available year-round that are devoted to Santa Claus and keeping tabs on his activities in his workshop. Many of these websites also include e-mail addresses, a modern version of the postal service letter writing, in which children can send Santa Claus e-mail."

Dressing up like Santa and imitating him provides are real live image for the children to see and touch. Parents encourage communication (letters), bonding times (on his lap), the children putting their hope in this man, and dreaming of him, his helpers, his sleigh and reindeer. The result of such extensive encouragement of a person (in this case, a child) to believe and trust in someone, is causing that believing child to engage in a form of worship. Just because it is only for one month of the year does not mean it does not count. If you decided to shoplift only during the Christmas season, that does not make it ok.

Worship is spiritual intimacy in the form of adoration, trust and closeness. When people worship something or someone other than God Almighty (even if only for one month) then they are giving of their soul and devotion to that one or thing spiritually. That is an example of a spiritual law. The worship or devotion to an idol (any object or being [other than God] that a person would set apart to adore and worship) is called idolatry.

One mother I located on the internet stated on her website: "Santa embodies a form of magic and love which is as real as anything else in the world." She continues, "It seems to me that a strong part of human behavior is to take the mystical and translate it into something accessible. Santa does precisely that. Santa is the mythological expression of a parent's selfless, joyful love for his children. A delightful gift, it seems to me, to not only be able to create magic, but to participate in it."
www.deafhomeschool.com/abundantliving/celebrations/santa.html

There is no need to create magical, accessible characters to represent your selfless, joyful love. Your children should be able to find love (and actually do experience more selfless, joyful love than you realize) during times of cuddling in your own lap, many times throughout the year. Yet some parents choose to try a less direct approach through pretending to be someone else (Santa Claus).

When people treat Santa like the North American most common tradition dictates they are actually (unknowingly) worshipping Santa.

You might be saying to yourself, "Wow! That is a pretty strong statement."

I agree; it is a startling thought that many people need take the time to ponder and learn about.

Let's look at how many people teach their children to treat Santa.

- ❖ Seek Santa, sit on his lap (a form of close adoration/worshiping Santa)
- ❖ Ask Santa for what you desire (praying to Santa)
- ❖ Write Santa a letter (a prayer to Santa)
- ❖ Believe that Santa is watching you (faith in Santa)
- ❖ Believe that Santa will answer your request (faith in and prayer to Santa)
- ❖ Set out milk and cookies for Santa (a sacrifice for Santa)
- ❖ Expect to wake up and find Santa has delivered to your home (faith in Santa)
- ❖ Thank Santa for answering and providing (gratitude to Santa)

Parents never look at Santa Claus like a god. They just pass on the tradition that they learned from their parents. They have no idea that they were (in innocent ignorance) encouraged to seek another god during the holiday season. They were led to dream of another source for their needs, and wants. That is seen by God as idolatry.

Since God loves people He made sure to warn them not to do the wrong act of idolatry. (See page 89 for Bible verses to support this matter.) Idolatry (worshipping something or someone) opens the worshipper's spirit up to be deeply affected by that something or someone that they are worshipping.

The revealing of this fact through this book is not meant to bring a condemning accusation against anyone. No guilt or shame should be involved in the discovery of the truth. Instead, one's heart should be lightened with happiness in finding knowledge that can bring opportunities to make better decisions.

I like how the book of 2 Corinthians in the Bible describes the type of corrective action I am hoping to inspire. 2 Corinthians (NIV) 7:10-11 "Godly sorrow (sorrow caused by God sending someone to correct you –constructive criticism) brings repentance that leads to salvation and leaves no regret, but worldly sorrow brings death (regret, depression). See what this godly sorrow has produced in you: what earnestness, what eagerness to clear yourselves, what indignation, what alarm, what longing, what concern, what readiness to see justice done. At every point you have proved yourselves to be innocent in this matter."

All these attitudes are powerful to bring about good change yet they must always be motivated by love and done in gentleness.

Warnings and correction help wise mature people only get wiser and more mature. I am confident that this will be true of most readers of this book.

It took the length of this book but finally the mystery bulb has been found!

The younger the children are, the easier it is to have fun just doing simple things. Their visit does not have to include a big production to be memorable.

God is the one true good God. He alone is the only one humans should worship. The only other spiritual overlord that humans are subject to outside of God Almighty is satan who is evil and cruel.

Yes, satan too is real and aims to devastate humans because he knows how much God loves them, and he hates God. So idolatry opens up a person's spirit to be affected by satan. This includes the worship of things like a tree, a statue, a famous pop star, a movie star or even an imaginary character like Santa Claus. The worshippers of anything that is not controlled and sent forth from God Almighty open themselves to the influence of satan. That is why God gave clear instruction in the Bible to stay away from such a spiritually dangerous condition.

Many families have decided that Jesus somehow did not make the holiday season special enough for them. Why? Jesus is actually real. He loves each of them very much, enough to die for them. Maybe it is because they know that believing in God means that they have to give up some things in life that seem fun. Careful study of the Bible shows that most of what God asked people to give up were things that would either eventually hurt them or leave them (body, soul or spirit) open to satan's attack. (See page 89 for Bible verses that support this matter.) Any good father would request or teach his children to be careful and stay away from harmful things. He would also train his children to be the very best they can be. When you choose to live for God and worship only Him then you have opened yourself up to the best Father you could ever have.

    One of the dimensions of the relationship that people were meant to have with God is that of a loving Father toward a faithful son. God is the most excellent Father. He seeks to guide each of His children to their highest potential. He provides for and trains His children. God's love runs deeper even than a parent toward a precious innocent child. Although He desires to protect and guide them He leaves them to make their own choices. When they choose to not listen to or to turn away from Him, it grieves Him. Jesus showed us how He feels when this happens. In the Bible book of Luke chapter 13 and verse 34, and also chapter 20 verse 41; also Matthew chapter 23 verse 37 Jesus cries out and weeps over God's people who have been sent a person from Him with messages from Him that would bring them peace, but they mistreated the messengers and would not listen to the message. He knew that meant that they would be stepping out of His protection, leaving them vulnerable to terrible destruction. If they would only trust Him, listen and obey they would be safe. (See pages 89 & 92 for Bible verses to support this matter.) It hurts a parent to see their children suffer. Similarly, God senses sorrow when people do not heed His warnings. Many people think that their poor decisions or lack of desire to live for God does not affect anyone else. But they are sadly mistaken because it negatively affects many others around them, plus, as we see above, it hurts our Heavenly Father's heart as well.

Children and younger siblings pick up quickly on attitudes we hold for certain traditions and stories.

It would not be wrong for parents to tell their children about the true Saint Nicholas who lived a good life. He did many acts of kindness just like God asks us to do. However, the story should not escalate from there to become fairy-tale like. We should use Saint Nicholas as an example of how wonderful it is to walk in a loving way with our neighbors and be the kind of loving, giving people that God tells us to be. All praise should go to God not to the saint who obeys God. God will make sure obedience is rewarded. We should make sure all praise goes to God who stirs our hearts to acts of love and obedience.

When children learn that God inspires people to do nice things for others and help others then they can also learn to trust Him to provide things they need through several different people and several different ways. God is our source for all we need to get wealth. (See page 89 for Bible verses that support this matter.) He provides health, wisdom, favor, guidance, and a means by which to get a job.

God is capable of providing much more than just money or tangible items. He can also provide peace, joy and hope for our souls. He heals the physical body as well as the mind and heart. So when we seek anything good God should always be our source. It is God who deserves each person's gratitude and respect.

If you have heard it said that living a good Christian life is boring, then the person that told you that must have had a limited concept of God. Many times God answers prayer according to the development of faith the one who prayed has. If the one who prayed has not developed their faith to stretch to believe for great things (such as miraculous healing - mental or physical, provision beyond their means, favor in they eyes of authorities, etc.) then God will only grant what their undeveloped faith could grasp.

God does not want people to be bored or live a dull life. He wants them to realize how exciting, fun and wonderful it is to be in love with Him. He hears prayers, rewards, and rescues in powerful and sometimes supernatural ways. (See page 90 for Bible verses that support this matter.) He also wants people to realize how dangerous it is to be seeking other gods or idols. The enemy, satan, works through idols or other things, and his goal is always to steal, kill and destroy. God Almighty wants to guard us from that. If people hold fast to God Almighty, love Him and seek Him as their source for everything then they will find true fulfillment and also be safe from the enemy's tricks.

The Bible records in John 10:10 "The thief (satan) comes only to steal and kill and destroy. I came that they may have life and have it in abundance."

This means that God not only wanted to provide us with protection and keep us alive, but He made a way for us to have a good life that is fulfilling and successful. There will still be some trials and troubles we will have to face, but He will be with us giving us what we need to make it through. He created each person with unique individual talents to do a specific mission in life. When people do what He made them to do with His help and guidance then they find success.

A life given to God is filled with trust in things you cannot see; happiness that goes deep; and a hope that cannot be shaken. Power that supersedes human strength is available in times of need. Peace and joy are available in times when life seems too hard to handle. A sound mind and stable character are results of time with God. God can be approached anytime. He provides all that is needed to be close to Him, anytime of the year, not just on holidays.

God tells us in His word how much He wants people to love Him and cling to Him. This keeps them safe plus they get to enjoy companionship with Him, a loving just God. When people go after other gods then they open their lives up to attack from satan, who hates them. Satan is the Father of lies. He is a thief of spiritual things and master of deception. When people go after other gods this also grieves God's heart, making Him angry. The relationship that God desires to have with His people is similar to a marriage relationship in that they spend time with each other, learning to love each other, trust each other and do special things for each other. (See page 90-91 for Bible verses that support this matter.) It also means that when His people worship other gods it is as if they have been unfaithful mates, cheating on their true love.

The God of Abraham, Isaac and Jacob; Father of Jesus Christ is the one true God. He desires people to love Him and worship Him only. He is the all-powerful God Who loves people and desires to protect them and strengthen them.

Many people reject this love because they do not believe in God. Others are not comfortable with being asked to change by leaving their comfort zone or leaving behind familiar traditions passed down from their families. As mentioned previously in this book, the revealing of spiritual facts through this book is not meant to bring a condemning accusation against anyone. No guilt or shame should be involved in the discovery of the truth. Instead, one's heart should be lightened with happiness in finding knowledge that can bring opportunities to make better decisions.

There are examples in the Bible of people much like people of today who had their own ways of doing things and they did not want to change. They did not want to even hear truth. They only wanted leaders to tell them things that sounded good. (See page 92). In the case of passing on the tradition of Santa Claus the children were lied to (knowingly) in an effort to make the season special.

The Bible states clearly in the book of Colossians in chapter 3 verses 9 and 10:
"Do not lie to one another, since you laid aside the old self with its evil practices and have put on the new self who is being renewed to a true knowledge according to the image of the One who created him."
Another Biblical book, Ephesians, chapter 4 verses 14-15, verse 25; says,
"As a result, we are no longer to be children, tossed here and there by waves, and carried about by every wind of doctrine, by the trickery of men, by craftiness in deceitful scheming; but speaking the truth in love, we are to grow up in all aspects into Him,"
"Therefore, laying aside falsehood, speak truth, each one of you, with his neighbor, for we are members of one another." (See page 92 for Bible verses that support this matter.)

When people do things that are wrong in God's eyes, then sometimes disasters and bad things happen. Most people are unaware that acts that God considers wrong remove God's protective covering over them. It is God's love for people that brings Him to warn them of danger. He is not the one that causes disasters. Instead it is either the people choosing to go against a spiritual law that they do not understand resulting in their calamity; or it is the work of the enemy, satan, who thrives on hurting people. As stated previously in this book, satan knows that people are valuable and precious to God. Since satan hates God, his way of hurting God is by attacking people. (See page 91 for Bible verses that support this matter.) So when people do things their own way, either through ignorance or purposefully choosing to ignore God's warnings and instructions, they are actually choosing to step out from under His protection. To get back under God's protective cover people must admit they were wrong, tell God they are sorry and then follow what God instructs them to do.

It is a beautiful thing, especially in God's eyes, when people come to the point where they admit they did wrong and they come tell Him sincerely that they are sorry. There is never any condemnation or shame in this humble act. God, the loving Father, simply uses it to show the one who did wrong what happens when they try to do things without His help and approval. Then He draws them close as if it never happened and puts them back on track to a safe and successful future.

The Bible is God's book of instruction and letter of love to people.

Psalms 34:12-16 In the New Living Translation of The Bible says, "Does anyone want to live a life that is long and prosperous? Then keep your tongue from speaking evil and your lips from telling lies. Turn away from evil and do good. Search for peace and work to maintain it. The eyes of the Lord watch over those who do right; His ears are open to their cries for help. But the Lord turns His face against those who do evil; He will erase their memory from the earth."

Psalms 34:21 In the New Living Translation of The Bible says, "Calamity will surley overtake the wicked, and those who hate the righteous will be punished." (See page 92-93 for more verses to support this matter.)

As a wrong act is forgiven and removed the Holy Spirit, whom God sends to help people, will come and help or strengthen people who have been weakened in their spirit or deceived by doing wrong acts (acts of idolatry, lying, and other wrong behavior or thoughts) unknowingly. Once set free from this deception of a wrong tradition people find a sweeter communion with God Almighty. They also are rewarded by Him as they choose to take a stand obeying His command to worship only Him. One of the best rewards will be a rich powerful Christmas season as has never been experienced before.

You can have control of the atmosphere in your home. Let it be an atmosphere of trust, love and fun.

If it has been unclear up to this point what the main objective of Way Five is, this is it: Settle in your heart the decision to gently and lovingly faze Santa Claus out of Christmas for you and your household. Consider what needs to happen to correct this situation of a tradition involving wrong acts of idolatry and lying that has been passed down from generation to generation.

As people go through this important transformation it is imperative that they keep in mind that condemnation and shame is not a part of turning from wrong to right. Deciding to turn from wrong and do the right thing should leave one realizing that they made the right decision and freedom, cleansing peace and joy are now on their horizon.

Now that that is understood here is what needs to take place. Not only do the adults who dreamed of Santa Claus and believed in him at one time need to sincerely tell God they are sorry (repent) for this act of idolatry now that they are aware of it, but all those who encouraged children (either their own or others) to believe in Santa need to sincerely tell God that they are sorry (repent) about leading little ones to do wrong (sin) as well.

Those who have been influential in causing innocent children to stumble in their understanding and knowledge of spiritual matters will be held responsible some day in heaven for the things they have passed on. The biblical book of Mark in chapter 9 verse 42 reads: "But whoever causes one of these little ones who believe in Me (Jesus) to stumble, it would be better for him if a millstone were hung around his neck and he were thrown into the sea."
Even telling them that Saint Nicholas died long ago but can be contacted is wrong in God's eyes. God forbids people to contact those who have died, other than Jesus.

Though the wrong act of believing in Santa or lying and getting others to believe in Santa was done in ignorance, it still was done and needs to be cleared off the record in Heaven. They must admit that they acted wrongfully in this situation and are sincerely sorry; then make the choice to not do it again. Immediately, they will be forgiven by God and cleansed from their wrong. It will be removed from the records in Heaven and never be remembered anymore by God, against whom the wrong act was committed. (See page 94 for a Bible verse that supports this matter.)

When Jesus willingly submitted Himself to be killed, His blood was the precious price He paid to make it possible for wrong acts to be erased in Heaven's record. This innocent blood is the only thing that completely removes the wrong acts recorded. There is nothing a person can do to earn the removal of wrong acts, and it does not depend on any feature, intelligence, race, education, social status, or even gender. All people have to do is admit they did wrong and sincerely ask God to forgive them as they make the decision to never willingly do that wrong again. Then in Heaven Jesus' blood that came out when He was cruelly killed will be shown to have completely erased forever the wrong act that was admitted to here on earth. It is a simple transaction yet very important for the relationship between God and each individual.

Once Heaven's records reveal that the individual was forgiven of this wrong act, which happens the moment that they repent, it is remembered by God no more, as if it never happened. The blood of Jesus is powerful and thorough in which people can fully trust to cleanse their records and spirit of any wrong. Now with a "clean slate" people can embark on the journey of enjoying a Christmas Season with a new perspective that includes a deeper sense of closeness with God Almighty.

If the thought of completely erasing Santa Claus from all your celebrations is still difficult for you to grasp, ask yourself this, "What I am holding onto? What am I willing to fight for in this made-up character who cannot hear, see, smell, taste, feel, or even care for me? What if in July I'm rushed to the hospital from a horrible car crash? Do I call out to Santa Claus? What would I say to my husband if he leaned over my hospital bed as I lay all bandaged from a head-on collision and said, 'I'll write Santa a letter asking him for help'? What makes Santa Claus so necessary in the Holiday celebrations?" It is probably all those things that Jesus stands for. He is the One Who really does care for you all year long and can help with any difficulty you may face.

Without the magical story of Santa Claus to tell, what can people do to develop imagination and good traditions? "Way One" through "Way Four" of this book give suggestions for some new traditions to be introduced and enjoyed for generations to come. Christmas really can be wonderful without Santa Claus even being mentioned. Better memories await your children's future, so let the Santa Claus tradition fade into history.

Kids can be entertaining by just being themselves.

For the first few years of breaking away from that tradition you may choose to read to your children and family members the children's Christmas book: **A Real Rich Christmas**, by Ami Keath, an adventure/mystery written for ages 7 and up (www.enlighteningeyes.com).

A good book to consider for the Christmas season this year and every year after is **The Purpose of Christmas** by Rick Warren (www.saddlebackresources.com)

    The Bible encourages us to dream of things above. It says that we are to think on good things. The biblical book of Philippians in chapter 4 verse 8 reads:
"Finally, brethren, whatever is true, whatever is honorable, whatever is right, whatever is pure, whatever is lovely, whatever is of good repute, if there is any excellence, and if anything worthy of praise, let your mind dwell on these things."
    It was God's wise design for the human brain to develop a good imagination. It is one of the tools useful for living the way that God desires people to live, for He calls His people to live by faith. Since faith is believing in what you cannot see, but instead what God promises will be; that takes a lot of dreaming and imagination.
The book of Hebrews in the Bible, chapter 11 verse 6 says, "But without faith it is impossible to please God. For he that comes to God must believe that He is and that He is rewarder of those that diligently seek Him."
    How does the Bible define faith?
    The biblical book of Hebrews in chapter 11 verse 1 states:
"Now faith is the substance of things hoped for, the evidence of things not seen."

    Our children would be well versed in imagination and trust if we just do what the Bible says. Each and every holiday would be special if we teach our children about Jesus. There are so many wonderful rich things to know about Jesus that our children would never run out of things to imagine or dream. They would also get stronger in their relationship with God. Their maturity level would increase as they learn to be content, loving, and giving instead of greedy and unsatisfied dreaming of that one present that they feel will complete their satisfaction for the holiday.
    Read the Bible for yourself and see how much God loves you. Learn how much there is in store for those who choose to

believe, love and live for God instead of turning to old traditions passed down that lead to lying and idolatry. Discover a whole realm of power so pure and so real; the power of sincere love for God and each other. Spiritual wisdom awaits those who are hungry for it.

Do not let the media and commercial pressure sway your choice to make the Christmas season one of truth and sincerity. Guard your children against the deceitfulness of the pretending that leads to idolatry and lying.

Remember to be motivated by love for God and love for others when people question your choice. Lovingly let them know about the dangers of pretending to seek anyone other than God for presents or meaning to any season. Be careful that you do not tell or encourage people to hate Santa. God is love, not hate. Inform them that the Almighty God of the universe is plenty exciting and desires all people to seek Him and no other. Do not by any means get angry with or criticize someone who does not agree with you. Pray for them in private to come to the knowledge of the truth. Once you have gently and lovingly told them what you know then it is the Holy Spirit's job to convict them and enlighten their hearts from within. (See page 93 for Bible verses that support this approach).

Let the children see only peaceful communication.

I have spent much of my life seeking God, yielding to Him and developing a relationship with Him. Those who diligently seek and pursue Him find Him. He rewards their pure sincere heart pursuit of Him. It is from this closeness with Him that I feel that I have received an insight into some of His ways and spiritual issues. When He shows me things that are not right in His eyes, then I have the responsibility to submit myself to be corrected in those areas then to warn others because I love them so that they too may have the opportunity to make the decision to turn from wrong acts (sin).

My mission I feel parallels somewhat to that of the mission found in the biblical book of Ezekiel. Ezekiel 3:17-21 "Son of man, I have made you a watchman to the house of Israel; therefore hear the word at My mouth and give them warning from Me. If I say to the wicked, 'You shall surely die', and you do not give him warning or speak to warn the wicked to turn from his wicked way, to save his life, the same wicked man shall die in his iniquity, but his blood I will require at your hand. Yet if you warn the wicked and he turn not from his wickedness or from his wicked way, he shall die in his iniquity, but you have delivered yourself. Again, if a righteous man turns from his righteousness (right doing and right standing with God) and some gift or providence which I lay before him he perverts into an occasion to sin and he commits iniquity, he shall die; because you have not given him warning, he shall die in his sin and his righteous deeds which he has done shall not be remembered, but his blood will I require at your hand. Nevertheless if you warn the righteous man not to sin and he does not sin, he shall surely live because he is warned; also you have delivered yourself from guilt."

Another similar situation that resembles my quest is found in the Biblical book of Malachi 2:5-7 "My covenant was with him, a covenant of life and peace, and I gave them to him; this called for reverence and he revered Me and stood in awe of My name. True instruction was in his mouth and nothing false was found on his lips. He walked with Me in peace and uprightness, and turned many from sin. For the lips of a priest ought to preserve knowledge, and from his mouth men should seek instruction – because he is the messenger of the Lord Almighty." (See page 93 for more Bible verses on this matter.)

That is a big responsibility. Yet it is not too heavy for me to bear because even though I am not perfect I trust that God will always provide all that I need to be able to do what He calls me to do.

So in sincere love I share this book that God inspired me to write with as many as I can. Please see the heart of God beckoning you and your family to come closer to Him and understand how according to His heart to celebrate holidays and how to live each moment of each day.

God blesses people with family and income to afford presents on special occasions. Let us not turn those blessings into a tradition that goes against the very loving God who provided them.

Instead launch out, make the right decision, and have a cleansing Christmas with new found freedom and friendship with Jesus, and those around you. You will see that Christmas can still be really fun and meaningful without Santa Claus.

A Picture of an Amazing Christmas Visit:

    Let us take a moment now to see what a Christmas could look like if someone was to enact with sincerity and cheerfulness all the five ways set forth in this book to celebrate the Christmas season. On approach to their place of residence it would be noticed that they enhanced their abode with a sparkling glow emanating from various colors of lights carefully and creatively chosen and set in just the right configurations. Friends next door would give a kind greeting as the resident came home returning the cordial wave confirming the acknowledgement of their newly started friendship. This causes one to be refreshed by the good natured atmosphere as opposed to drawing near to a dwelling surrounded by strangers that happen to live next door and coldly glance as the resident enters his driveway shut off from the neighbors' lives.

    Entering the front door, the visitors are welcomed in through a tunnel of glistening lit partitions that lead to a miniature dream land spread before them. Here they discover the wonder of a world in which the host's destiny is realized in full measure. The vision of success and fulfillment is intricately built to immaculately detailed specification. So many questions arise giving ample opportunity for the host to share thoughts and dreams with the visitors enabling them to draw closer in their relationship to and knowledge of the host. A sense of accomplishment and hope becomes apparent as the host explains plans to make it all come to pass. Think of what this would have looked like for someone like Walt Disney in his younger years.

    Walking into the kitchen for a hot cocoa the visitors spot a picture on the refrigerator of a special person (or animal). While studying it closely the host relates a touching story of how the subject of the picture was the one chosen this year to be visited and helped as one that was less fortunate. The memories gained from the encounter were rich and lasting. The photo serves to remind the host to pray for and even continue to visit and send gifts through the year to this person (or animal) who tugged at the host's heart. The account stirs the visitor to look into helping others as well.

Now with cocoa in hand the visitor follows the host into another room where a personalized calendar lays open awaiting new entries. The visitor is beckoned to mark their birthday, anniversary and any other dates they are aware of at the time that they consider special to them. Riddled with a rainbow of colorful marks and stickers where others have designated anticipated dates, the calendar is growing with opportunities for gift-giving all through the year. The heaviness of heaping all gifts to be bought all at one time is gone having been spread out through the rest of the year making each gift more feasible to afford. Delicious recipes and foods are shared as just another delightful part of getting together. Children that are visiting are directed to an area made ready for a fun craft to be assembled. They dive into the activity giddy with excitement coloring, cutting, pasting and folding materials into a work of art. Guarding it closely the children take pride in what they have done. They leave with not only a self-constructed gift, but the sense of accomplishment and memory of bringing it into form with their own hands.

The whole visit is so pleasant, even fun and beyond that to peacefully comfortable and meaningful because there is something deeper happening here that makes it such a worthwhile bonding time. The visitors recall their friend (the host) excitedly announcing a while ago, his discovery of Jesus and his decision to start living for Him. Since that time their friend has shown signs of humility that were rarely evident before. Depressive attitudes and negativity appear to be diminishing quickly being replaced by outward expressions of gratitude for even the smallest of things. His focus has been realigned to be set on others, with God being top of the list, instead of self. Benefitting richly from his new inner helper (the Holy Spirit) he is growing in areas of relationships that were difficult for him before. It is almost like an extra deposit of love and compassion has been downloaded in the host's heart. This is what makes the atmosphere of every visit with their changed friend a good one. This is what makes their friend experience such an amazing Christmas with many more to come in the future.

Display the truth with respect and honor.

The Most High God deserves no less.

Get to Know the Real Provider

If you were unable to find out how to become a child of God, it is quite simple yet a decision that changes your life. First of all, you must truly believe that God sent Jesus to earth; Jesus died for you; and then God, the Father, raised Him from the dead. Then just accept the free gift of admittance into God's household by asking forgiveness of any wrong things you have done and committing to live by the things Jesus taught about in the Bible. This involves making Jesus your Lord, your leader that you gratefully obey no matter what. After all, He wants what is best for you and knows all about every area of your life. This makes Him the best one to guide you to be the best you can be. Another benefit you have received is that you can ask the Holy Spirit, Who now lives in you, to help you with anything you might need. When the Holy Spirit speaks to you it is not by an audible voice. It is an impression clear and unmistakable in your mind or your spirit. It is like an awesome idea just pops into your head that you know you did not come up with on your own. Just quiet yourself down and listen to your heart. If you need help praying a prayer to accomplish all this, go to the end of this section. I have written a sincere example prayer you can pray.

As you are diligent to identify things in the Bible that Jesus instructed people to do and how to live then you will discover what a compassionate, fair and loving God He is. You will find yourself becoming more aware of His gentleness and profound wisdom. He draws you close to see His heart of tenderness for those that love Him. He rewards those that just let go of their own opinions and cravings to yield to His way of handling things that come up in their lives. Should you pursue getting to know Jesus more, you will encounter a relationship with Him that is the best relationship you have ever experienced. Since He is good, pure, loving and faithful He will not hurt you or have any wrong, evil motives in any of His plans for you and times with you. So reach out without reservation to Him and enjoy a loving companionship like you have never known before.

You may be familiar with the Bible verse John 3:16 (NAS), "For God so loved the world that He gave His only begotten Son, that whoever believes in Him should not die, but have eternal life." The verse immediately following states, "For God did not send His Son into the world to judge the world, but that the world should be saved through Him."

Did you notice in verse 16 why God sent His only Son? It was because He loved people of this world so much that He wanted to make a way for them to live forever with Him. In the small book of 1 John towards the end of the Bible we read in chapter 4 verse 9 (New American Standard version), "By this the love of God was manifested in us, that God has sent His only begotten Son into the world so that we might live through Him."
. He wants to save them from death. This includes death of relationships, death of dreams, death of physical bodies, death of careers, anything that brings destruction to the calling for which He created you. James 1:13-15 of the Bible says, "Let no one say when he is tempted, 'I am being tempted by God;' for God cannot be tempted by evil, and He Himself does not tempt anyone. But each one is tempted when he is carried away and enticed by his own lust. Then when lust has conceived, it gives birth to sin; and when sin is accomplished, it brings forth death." That is one of the things that Jesus was sent by Almighty God to save people from. He loves people enough to provide a way for them to have access to His strength to resist temptation and thus, not to sin. When someone invites Jesus to be the Lord of their life then He sends the Holy Spirit to live inside that person giving them His inner strength to stand strong in times of temptation.

Ephesians 2:3-5 explains, "Among them we too all formerly lived in the lusts of our flesh, indulging the desires of the flesh and of the mind, and were by nature children of wrath, even as the rest. But God, being rich in mercy, because of His great love with which He loved us, even when we were dead in our transgressions, made us alive together with Christ (by grace – unearned favor- you have been saved)." His motive towards people is a deep love. He cherishes us.

We find in Psalms many places where it reveals how loving, kind and merciful God is. Some of my favorite verses are Psalms 145:8-9, "The Lord is gracious and merciful; slow to anger and rich in love. The Lord is good to all, and His mercies are over all His works." Verses 17 through the first half of verse 20 of that same chapter continue to give us a small peek into our awesome God. "The Lord is righteous in all His ways, and kind in all His deeds. The Lord is near to all who call upon Him, to all who call upon Him in truth. He will fulfill the desire of those that fear Him; He will also hear their cry and will save them. The Lord keeps all who love Him."

If you have had a loved one suffer or be taken from you some time in your life and you are blaming God, remember that He is not an angry God carelessly punishing people. He lovingly provides each person with many warnings of wrong behavior that lead to danger and He sends many invitations to come to Him. If people choose not to listen, or feel their way is better, not understanding the spiritual dangers in their path, then His protection cannot cover them. He yearns for them to make the right choice but allows them to make their own decisions.

Psalm 81:8-14 (New Living Trans.), "Listen to Me, O My people, while I give you stern warnings, O Israel, if you would only listen to Me! You must never have a foreign god; you must not bow down before a false god. For it was I, the Lord your God, Who rescued you from the land of Egypt. Open your mouth, and I will fill it with good things. But no, My people would not listen. Israel did not want Me around. So I let them follow their own stubborn desires, living according to their own ideas. Oh, that My people would listen to Me! O, that Israel would follow Me, walking in My paths! How quickly I would then subdue their enemies. How soon My hands would be upon their foes."

Isaiah 55:6-7 (NAS) "Seek the Lord while He may be found; call upon Him while He is near. Let the wicked forsake his way, and the righteous man his thoughts; and let him return to the Lord, and He will have compassion on him; to our God, for He will abundantly pardon."

Psalms (NAS) 103:10-13 "He has not dealt with us according to our sins (we have not gotten the punishment we deserve), nor rewarded us according to our iniquities. For as high as the heavens are above the earth, so great is His lovingkindness toward those who fear (reverence) Him. As far as the east is from the west, so far has He removed our transgressions from us. Just as a father has compassion on his children, so the Lord has compassion on those who fear (reverence) Him."

Do you see now why so many people all through time have been so passionate about Jesus Christ? God, the Father, sent Him because of the deep love He has for His precious people that He created. He does not desire that anyone of them walk in dangerous paths. He wants them in close relationship with Him, talking with Him often and cheerfully following His excellent, pure and right paths. These paths could be rough at times but are rewarded richly with good things and a happy successful life. In addition to that God provides all that each person needs to make it through rough times infusing each of them with an inner peace that keeps them standing strong. By learning to trust completely in this faithful all-powerful God, each person finds a freedom that is a never ending supply of hope and strength.

If you are ready to turn toward Jesus and allow Him to welcome you into His spiritual kingdom right now as you live the rest of your life on earth for Him, making Him your Lord, then here is a real prayer you can pray if you pray it sincerely. Pray it out loud proving to yourself that you really mean it and are not ashamed. The devil cannot read your thoughts so let him hear this that will be bad news for him. (See page 94 to find Bible verses that support this idea).

PRAYER

"Jesus, please make Yourself real to me. I believe that You died for me and God raised You from the dead. And from this point on I want to live my life for You the way You instruct me to live. I am sorry for all the things in my life that I have done that are not right in Your eyes. (Try to be specific as you tell Him sincerely that you are sorry for each one that you remember; example stealing anything, being mean to people and not forgiving them, lying about something or someone, being unfaithful to a mate, cheating on a test, and so on). Please forgive me of these things. Come live in my heart and let Your Holy Spirit live in me as well to help me, comfort me and teach me. I thank You for removing all my sins and accepting me into Your kingdom giving me access to all I will need, to do what You ask me to do. I pray this in your Name, Jesus Christ, my Lord. Amen."

When you have prayed this prayer, mark this as your spiritual birthday. What a day to get excited about and celebrate! Do not hesitate to bring it up when thoughts of doubt arise or the enemy, satan, tries to bring up things in your mind that you have already told God that you are sorry for. Those things are gone forever and you are now a child of God, welcomed into His household with granted access to Heaven when you die. You now have within you God's Holy Spirit as well Who gives you spiritual wisdom and insight like you never had before. You can find out from Him if you are doing what you have been called and formed to do. This is important because it is only when you are doing your calling that you will truly be happy and successful. You are in good standing with Almighty God so you can talk with Him whenever you desire. His protection over you is established plus you and He are at peace with each other. There are so many more wonderful things that have happened to you today for taking this step, as you will find out when you read the Bible. One example is Psalms 103 which lists some benefits you will want to check out. Congratulations; the angels are celebrating your decision and if you let me know about it, I will celebrate also.

To my Heavenly Father - God of Abraham, Isaac and Jacob, Father of my sweet Savior and Lord, Jesus Christ; the One through Whom I live;

Thank You, for giving me all I needed to do this work that You called me to do.

May all who read it see the love that came from You to them. May they come to know You as the powerful, real and loving God that I have discovered You are. I especially ask You to let my children see my devotion to You in humble gratitude for all You do for and through me. Let them realize that You are more real than even things that they can see with their eyes and feel with their hands. From the way I respect You and all things that pertain to You, let my children develop a reverence for You that pleases Your heart.

I love You so much, Jesus. Knowing that You eagerly await communication with Your people I quickly push aside traditions and busy work that would distract me from You. Why would I waste my time on fantasy when You, the Almighty God of the universe watch for me to approach Your glorious throne through my sincere pursuit of You? Each moment that I get to quiet myself and just listen for You is a moment well spent.

May the people of the United States of America and even the whole world turn away from spiritually and physically harmful things and turn toward You. May they be enlightened in a loving way to be able to see that You alone are God and that You love them deeply. Then they will experience Your goodness and never want to go back to their own way of doing things.

To You, my King and my friend, be praise and honor and glory forever.

Love,
Ami Keath

"I have kept my feet from every evil path so that I might obey Your word. I have not departed from Your laws for You Yourself have taught me. How sweet are Your words to my taste, sweeter than honey to my mouth! I gain understanding from Your precepts; therefore I hate every wrong path."
Psalms 119:101-104

Bible Verses Previously Referenced

Page 36   Proverbs 15:13 & 15 "A joyful heart makes a cheerful face, but when the heart is sad, the spirit is broken…All the days of the afflicted are bad, but a cheerful heart has a continual feast."

Page 62   Isaiah 42:17 "They shall be turned back; they shall be utterly put to shame, who trust in idols, who say to the molten images, 'You are our gods'."

Exodus 20:23 "You shall not make anything to be with (alongside) Me, - gods of silver or gods of gold you shall not make for yourselves." NKJ version

Exodus 20:23 "You shall not make other gods besides Me; gods of silver or gods of gold, you shall not make for yourselves."

Psalms 24:3-4 "Who may ascend into the hill of the Lord? Who may stand in His holy place? He who has clean hands and a pure heart, who has not lifted up his soul to an idol, nor sworn deceitfully."

Matthew 4:9-10 "and he (satan) said to Him (Jesus), 'All these things I will give You if You will fall down and worship me.' Then Jesus said to him, 'Away with you, satan! For it is written, 'You shall worship the Lord your God and Him only you shall serve.''"

Page 65   Proverbs 8:32-36 "Now therefore, listen to Me (Jesus personified as wisdom), my children, for blessed are those who keep My ways. Hear instruction and be wise and do not disdain it. Blessed is the man who listens to Me, watching daily at My gates, waiting at the posts of My doors. For whoever finds Me finds life and obtains favor from the Lord; but he who sins against Me wrongs his own soul; all those who hate Me love death."

Page 66   "Deuteronomy 8:17-18 "Otherwise, you may say in your heart, 'My power and the strength of my hand made me this wealth.' But you shall remember the Lord your God, for it is He who is giving you power to make wealth, that He may confirm His covenant which He swore to your fathers, as it is to this day."

Page 67   Psalms (NAS) 103:2-14, 17-18, "Bless the Lord, O my soul, and forget none of His benefits. Who pardons all your iniquities, Who heals all of your diseases; Who redeems your life from the pit; Who crowns you with lovingkindness and compassion; Who satisfies your years with good things, so that your youth us renewed like the eagle. The Lord performs righteous deeds, and judgments for all who are oppressed. He made known His ways to Moses, His acts to the sons of Israel. The Lord is compassionate and gracious, slow to anger and abounding in lovingkindness. He will not always strive with us; nor will He keep His anger forever. He has not dealt with us according to our sins, nor rewarded us according to our iniquities. For as high as the heavens are above the earth, so great is His lovingkindness toward those that fear Him. As far as the east is from the west, so far has He removed our transgressions from us. Just as a father has compassion on his children, so the Lord has compassion on those who fear (reverence) Him…But the lovingkindness of the Lord is from everlasting to everlasting on those who fear Him, and His righteous to children's children; to those who keep His covenant, and remember His precepts to do them."

Page 68   Exodus 34:12-14 of The Bible says, "Watch yourself that you make no covenant with the inhabitants of the land into which you are going, lest it become a snare in your midst. But rather, you are to tear down their altars and smash their sacred pillars and cut down their wooden symbols of gods –for you shall not worship any other god, for the Lord, whose name is Jealous, is a jealous God."

Page 68/69   Jeremiah 2:17-19 "'Have you not brought this on yourselves by forsaking the Lord your God when He led you in the way? Now why go to Egypt to drink water from Shihor? And why go to Assyria to drink water from the River? Your wickedness will punish you; your backsliding will rebuke you. Consider them and realize how evil and bitter it is for you when you forsake the Lord your God and have no awe of Me', declares the Lord, the Lord Almighty."

James 4:4-5 "…Do you not know that friendship with the world is enmity (enemy behavior) with God? Whoever therefore wants to be a friend of the world makes himself and enemy of God. Or do you think that the scripture says in vain, 'The Spirit who dwells in us yearns jealously?'

The Bible states when God's people went after other gods he saw it as them playing the harlot.

Jeremiah 3:14 "Return, faithless people, 'declares the Lord, 'for I am your husband. I will choose you one from a town and two from a clan – and bring you to Zion."

Jeremiah 31:32 "It will not be like the covenant I made with their forefathers when I took them by the hand to lead them out of Egypt, because they broke My covenant, though I was a husband to them,' declares the Lord."

Isaiah 1:21 "How the faithful city has become a harlot, she who was full of justice! Righteousness once lodged in her, but now murderers."

2 Corinthians 11:2-4 "I am jealous for you with a godly jealousy. I promised you to one husband, to Christ, so that I might present you as a pure virgin to Him. But I am afraid that just as Eve was deceived by the serpent's cunning, your minds may somehow be led astray from your sincere and pure devotion to Christ. For if someone comes to you and preaches a Jesus other than the Jesus we preached, or if you receive a different spirit from the one you received, or a different gospel from the one you accepted, you put up with it easily enough."

Proverbs 13:5 "A righteous man hates lying, but a wicked man is loathsome and comes to shame."

Proverbs 26:28 "A lying tongue hates those who are crushed by it, and a flattering mouth works ruin."

Page 69   Isaiah 30: 9-11 "For this is a rebellious people, false sons, Sons who refuse to listen to the instruction of the Lord; who say to the seers, 'You must not see visions', and to the prophets, 'You must not prophesy to us what is right, speak to us pleasant words, prophesy illusions. Get out of the way, turn aside from the path, Let us hear no more, about the Holy One of Israel.'"

Romans 12:9-14 "Let love be genuine. Abhor what is evil; hold fast to what is good. Love one another with brotherly affection. Outdo one another in showing honor. Do not be slothful in zeal, be fervent in spirit, serve the Lord. Rejoice in hope, be patient in tribulation, be constant in prayer. Contribute to the needs of the saints and seek to show hospitality. Bless those that persecute you; bless and do not curse them."

Amos 5:14-15 "Seek good and not evil that you may live; so Yahweh, God of Hosts will be with you...Hate evil, love good; establish justice in your gates."

Page 70 & 65 Psalms 97:10-11 "Let those who love the Lord hate evil, for He guards the lives of His faithful ones and delivers them from the hand of the wicked. Light is shed upon the righteous and joy on the upright in heart."

Proverbs 13:13 "He who despises the word will be destroyed, but he who fears the commandment will be rewarded."

Psalms 119:32, 45-46 (NIV) "I run in the path of Your commands, for You have set my heart free; ...I will walk about in freedom for I have sought out Your precepts. I will speak of Your statutes before kings, and will not be put to shame."

Psalms 40:4-5 "Blessed is the man who makes the Lord his trust, and does not respect the proud, nor such as turn aside to lies. Many, O Lord, my God, are Your wonderful works which You have done; and Your thoughts toward us cannot be recounted to You in order; If I would declare and speak of them, they are more than can be numbered."

Page 70 & 65   Proverbs 19:23 (NIV), "The fear of the Lord leads to life; then one rests content, untouched by trouble."

Page 72   1John 1:9 (NAS) "If we confess our sins, He is faithful and righteous to forgive us our sins and to cleanse us from all unrighteousness."

Page 76   2 Timothy 2:25-26 (NIV) "Those who oppose him he must gently instruct, in the hope that God will grant them repentance leading them to the knowledge of the truth, and they will come to their senses and escape from the trap of the devil, who has taken them captive to do his will."

2 Timothy 2:24-26 (NIV) "And the Lord's servant must not quarrel; instead he must be kind to everyone; able to teach, not resentful. Those who oppose him he must gently instruct, in the hope that God will grant them repentance leading them to the knowledge of the truth, and they will come to their senses and escape from the trap of the devil, who has taken them captive to do his will."

Page 78   Proverbs 24:11-12 (NIV) "Rescue those being led away to death; hold back those staggering toward slaughter. If you say, 'But we knew nothing about this,' does not He who weighs the heart perceive it? Does not He who guards your life know it? Will He not repay each person according to what he has done?"

James 5:19-20 "My brothers, if one of you should wander from the truth, and someone should bring him back, remember this: Whoever turns a sinner from the error of his way will save him from death and cover over a multitude of sins."

Ephesians 5:3, 5-11 "But among you there must not be even a hint of sexual immorality, or any kind of impurity, or any kind of greed, because these are improper for God's holy people. For of this you can be sure: No immortal, impure or greedy person – such a man is an idolater- has any inheritance in the kingdom of Christ and of God. Let no one deceive you with empty words, for because of such things God's wrath comes on those who are disobedient. Therefore, do not be partakers with them. For you were once darkness, but now you are light in the Lord. Live as children of light (for the fruit of the light consists in all goodness, righteousness and truth) and find out what pleases the Lord. Have nothing to do with the fruitless deeds of darkness, but rather expose them."

2 Timothy 4:2-4 (NIV) "Preach the Word; be prepared in season and out of season; correct, rebuke and encourage with great patience and careful instruction. For the time will some when men will not put up with sound doctrine. Instead, to suit their own desires, they will gather around them a great number of teachers to say what their itching ears want to hear. They will turn their ears away from the truth and turn aside to myths."

Page 86   Romans 10:9-10 (NAS) "that if you confess with your mouth Jesus as Lord, and believe in your heart that God raised Him from the dead, you shall be saved. For with the heart man believes, resulting in righteousness, and with the mouth he confesses, resulting in salvation."

Gratitude

Thank you, Saginaw Animal Control of Saginaw, Texas for allowing me to photograph some of your current resident animals. Their pictures are found on pages 32-33.

Thank you, James and Marta Sobel for the use of your home, decorations and daughters for some of the pictures. Their pictures are found on pages 11, 37, 38, 40, 51, 55 and 82.

Thank you, my friends and family for allowing me to photograph you.
Sang on pages 8 and 50;
Don on pages 21, 23, 43 and 63;
Angel on page 30;
Danny on pages 64, 71, 74 and 77;
Michelle and Miguel on page 66;
Yoanna, Jessica, Courtney, Chelsie, and my niece, Ami Christina Keren on pages 11, 37, 38, 40 and 51.

Thank you, my sons, Jesse and Jonathan, for cheerfully helping with and posing for many of the pictures for this book. I pray your smiles warm the hearts of all those that see them as they do my own heart that cherishes you both. Their pictures are found on pages 6, 25, 30-33, 64, 71, 74 and 77.

Thank you, Autumn Leaves of Flower Mound (assisted living facility) for allowing me to take pictures of my sons and my mother for this book. Their pictures are found on page 31. My mother is much happier now as she went to be with Jesus face to face a few months after these pictures were taken.

Thank you, Bethany, Brooke, and Hannah (on page 29) for sending me your picture to use.